W9-BDI-972

Bobbie Kalman

 Crabtree Publishing Company

www.crabtreebooks.com

Created by Bobbie Kalman

Dedicated by Samantha Crabtree
For Jeremy Payne

Author and Publisher
Bobbie Kalman

Editorial director
Niki Walker

Editor
Kathryn Smithyman

Copy editor
Molly Aloian

Art director
Robert MacGregor

Design
Bobbie Kalman
Katherine Kantor
Samantha Crabtree

Production coordinator
Heather Fitzpatrick

Illustrations
Barbara Bedell: pages 11, 16, 22, 25, 27
Tiffany Wybouw: pages 14, 15, 30

Special thanks to
Margaret Nacsa, Allison Vernal, Alexis Gaddishaw, Robin Turner,
Sophie Izikson, Martin Izikson, David Kanters, Sara Paton, Andrew Key,
Chantelle Styres, Tiffany Styres, Jacquelyn Labonté, Erica Olarte,
Jeremy Payne, Ivor Selimović, and Adam Vok

Consultants
Valerie Martin, Registered Nutrition Consultant,
    International Organization of Nutrition Consultants
Ellen Brown, Founding Food Editor of USA Today
    and author of several best-selling cookbooks

Photographs
All photographs by Bobbie Kalman except the following:
Marc Crabtree: back cover (top right), page 31 (top right,
    bottom left, and middle)
Other images by Comstock, PhotoDisc, Image Club Studio Gear,
    and Digital Stock

Food preparation
Valerie Martin
Kathryn Smithyman
Margaret Nacsa

Digital prepress
Embassy Graphics

Printer
Worzalla Publishing

Crabtree Publishing Company
www.crabtreebooks.com   1-800-387-7650

PMB 16A	612 Welland Avenue	73 Lime Walk
350 Fifth Avenue	St. Catharines	Headington
Suite 3308	Ontario	Oxford
New York, NY	Canada	OX3 7AD
10118	L2M 5V6	United Kingdom

Cataloging-in-Publication Data
Kalman, Bobbie
  Lunch munch / Bobbie Kalman.
    p. cm. -- (Kid power)
Includes index.
Explores why and how to have a delicious and healthy lunch
through nutrition facts and easy recipes for nourishing foods.
  ISBN 0-7787-1251-6 (RLB) -- ISBN 0-7787-1273-7 (pbk.)
  1. Luncheons--Juvenile literature. [1. Luncheons. 2. Food habits.
3. Cookery.] I. Title. II. Series.
  TX735.K35 2003
  641.5'3--dc21
                                                          2003001793
                                                          LC

CONTENTS

Nutritious lunches	4
Water bodies	6
The food groups	8
Be careful when you cook!	10
Cooking terms	11
Autumn Soup	12
Apple-Cheddar Muffins	14
Super Salad	16
Garlic Chicken Breasts	18
Zesty Rice or Pasta Salad	20
Potato Boats	22
Beautiful Bean Salad	24
Pita Sandwiches	26
Wrapping it up	28
What do I pack for lunch?	30
Active at lunchtime	31
Glossary and Index	32

NUTRiTiOUS LUNCHES

When you're at school, you probably can't wait for your lunch break. It's a chance to meet with your friends and refuel your body. After concentrating on your morning classes, you need more **energy**. Energy is the power your body needs to function. Your body gets energy from **nutritious** foods. Do you eat a lot of **processed** foods for lunch? Processed foods have been treated with chemicals that can harm you. Is a hot dog, a bag of chips, and a soda your idea of a meal? If so, you probably feel tired by the end of the day because your body is missing the things it needs to stay energized. Try making your lunch—even a couple of times a week—following the recipes in this book. They include a variety of foods made from fresh ingredients, which are better for you than processed foods are.

How to be healthy
- Drink plenty of water (see pages 6-7).
- Choose a variety of foods each day.
- Eat fresh fruits and vegetables every day.
- Read the labels on the packaging of processed foods to learn what they really contain. If you can't pronounce the ingredients, don't eat the food!
- Stock your house with healthy foods and get rid of foods that are loaded with fat, salt, and sugar.
- Eat at fast-food restaurants less often.
- **Downsize** your meals, or make them smaller, instead of **supersizing** them, or making them bigger.
- Take part in physical activity every day.
- Make health a family affair!

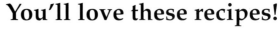

You'll love these recipes!

The kids in this book had fun making our lunch recipes, but they enjoyed the results even more! They loved the foods and were surprised at how delicious nutritious foods can taste.

You'll love them, too. Try these recipes with your family, and get everyone involved in healthy eating and in being active. You'll all feel great!

4

Nutrients in your food

Nutrients are substances in foods that your body needs. The seven essential nutrients are: water, carbohydrates, proteins, fats, vitamins, minerals, and enzymes. Your body needs all seven nutrients to work at its best. Eating a variety of foods and drinking plenty of water gives your body and brain maximum power.

Proteins

Proteins are your body's building blocks. They are found in meat, fish and seafood, eggs, milk and soy products, and **legumes**, or dried beans. There are two types of proteins: **complete** and **incomplete**. Complete proteins are in meat, eggs, and milk products. Incomplete proteins are found in beans and grains. When you combine some incomplete proteins, you get a complete protein. Eating a bean salad with whole-grain bread, or brown rice with beans, turns these foods into complete proteins.

Good fats and bad fats

You need fats to make new cells and to **absorb**, or take in, certain vitamins. Fats contained in olive oil, fish, and nuts are good for you. Other fats, such as those found in most processed foods, stop your cells from growing normally. These fats harm your body.

Enzymes

Enzymes are found in all fresh fruits and vegetables, especially in **organic** foods. They are needed by your **digestive** and **metabolic** systems to break down food so your body can absorb the nutrients it needs.

Carbohydrates

Carbohydrates are your body's main source of energy. There are three kinds—**simple**, **complex**, and **fiber**. Some are better for you than others. Simple carbohydrates are found in sugar and in white-flour products such as cake. They turn to fat quickly in your body. They are also found in fruits and in some vegetables, but these foods also contain fiber and other nutrients your body can use. Whole-grain foods, such as whole-wheat bread and many vegetables, contain complex carbohydrates. These foods release energy more slowly than simple carbohydrates do, so you feel energized for a longer time. They also contain fiber, which helps remove wastes from your body.

Vitamins

Vitamins are in all fresh foods. Cooking destroys many vitamins, so it is important to eat some **raw**, or uncooked, vegetables and fruits each day. Vitamins such as A, C, D, E, and K are essential to your body. They are also important in maintaining a healthy **immune system**, which fights diseases and keeps you from getting sick. Your immune system also helps you heal when you are sick or injured.

Minerals

Minerals include calcium, iron, potassium, magnesium, and zinc. They are as important as vitamins. Calcium, for example, helps build your bones. It is found in milk, meat, almonds, and green vegetables such as broccoli.

WATER BODIES

Water is the most important nutrient—you could not live without it for more than five days! 60 to 75 percent of your body is water. Your bones are 22 percent water, your muscles are 70 percent water, your blood is 83 percent water, and your brain is 75 percent water. Without water, your brain, muscles, bones, organs, and **metabolism** stop working! Your metabolism helps change the food you eat into energy.

How your body uses water

Your body's water supply:
- controls your body temperature
- keeps your skin healthy and smooth
- develops your muscles
- helps **lubricate**, or moisten, your food so you can digest it
- lubricates your eyes, nose, mouth, and every joint in your body so you can move
- carries nutrients, energy, and information to and from your cells
- helps your body get rid of wastes

The dangers of dehydration

Dehydration means losing water from your body. Being dehydrated can be dangerous! When you are dehydrated, your temperature rises, and your body loses minerals such as sodium and potassium. You can become sick from losing too much water. Dehydration is especially dangerous in hot weather or when you're physically active. Most people are slightly dehydrated all the time and don't even know it. Drink water throughout the day—before you feel thirsty. If you are thirsty, you are already dehydrated!

The best drink by far!

Many people drink sodas when they are thirsty, but they are doing the opposite of what their bodies need. Sodas contain caffeine, which takes water out of your body instead of adding water to it. Each can of soda also contains phosphorous and nine teaspoons of sugar! Too much phosphorous and caffeine can rob your bones of calcium, so if you are drinking sodas every day, your bones may be getting thinner! Vegetable juices, teas, and fruit juices add water to your body, but some contain sugar or salt. The best way to keep your body hydrated is to drink plenty of pure water!

Dehydration warning signs

Do you know the warning signs of dehydration? You might be dehydrated if you...
- are extremely thirsty
- are extremely hungry
- feel light-headed or dizzy
- feel hot
- are unable to concentrate
- have a dry mouth
- feel extremely tired
- are unusually clumsy
- have muscle spasms
- have a headache
- are short of breath
- have a rapid pulse
- have blurred vision
- have pain at the back of your ankles

Drink plenty of water!

You should try to drink at least 6-8 glasses of water a day. This amount sounds like a lot, but these tips can help you drink the water you need.

- Drink one to two glasses of water as soon as you get up in the morning. Add a squirt of lemon juice to your first glass to get your digestive system going. On a cold day, sip some hot water flavored with lemon.
- Sip—don't gulp—a half glass of water every 30 minutes, even when you do not feel thirsty.
- Always drink water before and after exercise. Do not drink ice-cold water or cold liquids when your body is very hot.
- Drink plenty of water when you are working in front of a computer. Computers can dehydrate you quickly.
- If you feel very hungry, you may be thirsty. Drink a glass of water and then see if you are still hungry.
- To make water taste more delicious, flavor it with fresh fruit or vegetable slices, as shown on this page.

2 To make **Orange Water**, wash an orange and cut it in half with its rind on. Cut it again into quarters and then slice the quarters into thirds. Use half an orange to flavor a jug of water. Do not squeeze the orange juice into the water—just drop the pieces into the jug. Allow the water to stand for about 30 minutes. You can refill the jug once using the same orange pieces. Discard the orange pieces after about six hours.

1 To make **Strawberry Water**, wash and slice five or six strawberries and add the pieces to a bottle or pitcher of water. Use one sliced berry to flavor a single glass of water. Allow a half hour for the strawberries to flavor the water. Drink the water within six hours and then throw the berries away.

3 To make **Cucumber Water**, wash a cucumber and peel it if it is too waxy. If not, then leave on the peel and slice five or six pieces from it. Allow the cucumber to flavor the water for a half hour. Take the flavored water to school in a drinking bottle.

THE FOOD GROUPS

There are four main **food groups**, or types of food: grain products, vegetables and fruits, milk and **alternatives**, and meat and alternatives. Alternatives are foods that contain the same type of nutrients as those found in certain other foods. Soy beverage, for example, is a milk alternative. Eating foods from different food groups provides your body with a wide variety of nutrients. Your body needs more grains and vegetables and fruits than it needs milk and meat products, however, so eat more from the two food groups on this page. Try to eat as little as possible of the "foods" mentioned in the blue box on page 9.

Vegetables and fruits

Vegetables and fruits are some of the best foods you can eat. They're packed with vitamins and minerals and also contain enzymes. Fruits and vegetables are high in fiber and low in fat. They give you a lot of energy and make you feel full. Have several kinds of fruits and vegetables each day and make sure you eat some of them raw. Remember that french fries, potato chips, and onion rings are not vegetables—they are mostly salt and fat.

Grain products

Your body needs a lot of grains. Some grains are better choices than others, however. Foods made with whole grains, such as whole-wheat bread, rice, and pasta, have a lot of nutrients, including fiber. They'll keep you powered for hours! **Refined**, or processed, grains are not as good for you. They include white rice and flour and foods made from these grains, such as bread, cakes, crackers, and cereals. Refined grains have had their most nutritious parts removed. They act like simple sugars in your body and do not give you long-lasting energy. A simple health rule is always to eat whole grains.

whole-wheat bread

white bread

8

Milk products and alternatives

Milk and dairy products provide you with protein, vitamins, and minerals such as calcium. Eating or drinking a milk product every day can also help you maintain a healthy weight. Milk alternatives such as soy beverages and cheeses are rich in protein and calcium, just as milk products are. Whether you choose milk products, soy products, or both, read the labels to see how much fat and sugar they contain. Also beware of artificial colors, flavors, and sweeteners that are used in some milk products. They are harmful to your body.

milk cheese

soy beverage

tofu

milk

soy cheese

milk cheese

Meat, fish, and alternatives

Meat and fish are great sources of protein, vitamins, and minerals. Fish such as salmon and sardines are especially good for you. Some people do not eat meat or fish, however. They choose alternatives such as eggs, a combination of beans and rice, or soy products such as tofu. Eggs are a wonderful food because they contain important nutrients that are hard to find in other foods. Almonds and peanuts are also considered to be meat alternatives because they contain protein and calcium.

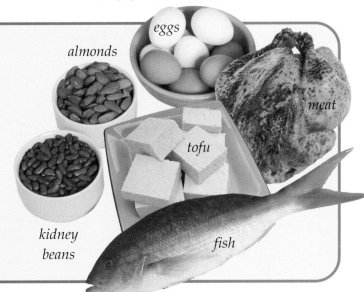

eggs

almonds

meat

tofu

kidney beans

fish

Not part of the four groups

Some foods don't fit into the four food groups. They get lumped together in a group of "other foods." The only healthy foods that belong to this group are good fats such as nuts and olive oil. Most of the "other foods" in this group shouldn't even be called foods because they have very few nutrients. "Junk foods" such as candy, cake, chips, and soda contain **empty calories**, which make you gain weight while starving your body at the same time. When you eat empty calories, your body wants you to keep eating because it is not getting the nutrients it needs. Junk foods may give you a burst of energy, but it doesn't last long! You'll feel tired soon after you eat them. Junk foods also contain a lot of artificial ingredients, too, such as sweeteners. Recent studies show that these ingredients cause many diseases, including liver disease, kidney disease, and cancer.

BE CAREFUL WHEN YOU COOK!

Cooking is fun, but it can also be dangerous if you are not careful. When you are using the oven, stove, a knife, or a food processor, make sure there is an adult in the kitchen with you. Accidents such as burns and cuts can happen quickly! **Allergies** are another common food-related problem. Before you start cooking, have an adult who knows your allergies check over each recipe's ingredients. Some foods may contain hidden ingredients such as nut oils. If you are allergic to nuts, be careful to read the labels on foods such as dried fruits and seeds. Nut oils can be found in many processed foods.

More safety tips

- Before and after handling food, wash with detergent and water all the surfaces on which you are working, such as cutting boards and countertops.
- Then wash your hands. Always wash your hands with soap and warm water after handling eggs and raw meat. When washing up, also include the backs of your hands, your fingertips and nails, and between your fingers, as well as your palms. How long do you wash your hands? As you soap your hands, sing the Happy Birthday song. Do not stop soaping until you have finished the song. Then rinse with warm water.
- Be sure to wash any raw vegetables and fruits thoroughly before you cook or eat them.
- Always wear oven mitts (shown right) when you handle anything in the oven.

- Turn the handles of pots and pans away from the edge of the stove so you do not accidentally knock them and spill hot food on yourself or others.
- If your hair is long, tie it back so that it does not touch the food or get caught while you are cooking.

COOKING TERMS

When using the recipes in this book, you may see some cooking **terms**, or special words, that aren't familiar to you. The pictures shown here illustrate some of these terms. The recipes also include metric measurements in brackets. The letter "l" stands for liter, and the letters "ml" mean milliliter. When you see the words **teaspoon**, **tablespoon**, or **cup** without metric amounts beside them, you can use a regular cup, teaspoon, or tablespoon from your kitchen. In fact, many of the ingredients in this book do not have to be exact. We use terms such as **sprinkle**, **dash**, **drizzle**, **pinch**, and **handful**. When you see these words, you can use a bit more or less of an ingredient.

purée: *blend food into a smooth paste*

slice, chop, dice: *cut food into even pieces*

mince, press: *squeeze food such as garlic through a press*

grease: *rub a pan with oil or butter so food won't stick*

simmer: *cook gently so food bubbles but does not boil*

sauté: *stir while cooking over medium heat*

whisk together: *blend well by using a whisk or a fork*

grate: *rub an ingredient against a grater*

toothpick test: *check to see if food is dry in center*

blend: *add ingredients while stirring*

handful: *an amount that fits in your hand*

sprinkle: *scatter solid or liquid particles over food*

11

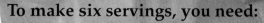

AUTUMN SOUP

This delicious soup is perfect on a chilly autumn afternoon, but it tastes great in any weather. It has a vibrant orange color because it contains **beta-carotene**, a nutrient that is good for your eyes. You can choose to make a thick or a creamy soup. To feel warm all afternoon, take this soup to school in a Thermos or enjoy it at home with your family or friends.

To make six servings, you need:
- 2 cups (500 ml) butternut squash
- 1 tablespoon (15 ml) vegetable oil
- 1 cup (250 ml) diced onions
- 1 teaspoon (5 ml) peeled, chopped fresh gingerroot or bottled gingerroot purée
- 1 clove minced garlic
- 2 cups (500 ml) chopped carrots
- ½ green or red pepper, chopped
- 4 cups (1 liter) vegetable or chicken stock (broth)
- 1 cup (250 ml) apple juice
- juice of 1 orange
- handful of fresh parsley or cilantro
- 1 teaspoon (5 ml) salt

1 Buy squash that is already peeled and cut into chunks. Squash is very hard to cut, so ask an adult to cut it into even smaller pieces for your soup.

2 In a large pot, heat the oil on medium heat and sauté the onions for 2-3 minutes, or until they look clear. Add the ginger and garlic and cook for another minute.

3 Stir in the carrots, squash, peppers, stock, apple and orange juice, and parsley or cilantro. Add salt.

You can make stock by stirring a chicken or vegetable bouillon cube into four cups of warm water.

12

4 On medium-high heat, bring the soup to a boil and then let it simmer for about 30 minutes, or until the carrots and squash are soft. Stir the soup often and ask an adult to test the vegetables to see if they are cooked. Allow the soup to cool until it is lukewarm.

This recipe makes enough soup to feed 4-6 people at once or give you a week's worth of lunches. Freeze individual portions of the soup to use as you need them.

5 When the soup is cool, spoon it into a blender or food processor. You may have to do this two or three times to purée all the soup, so have a big bowl ready to hold the portions you have blended. Return the purée to the pot and reheat.

6 If you enjoy a thick soup, serve it with a slice of whole-grain bread. You can **garnish**, or make the soup look more appetizing, with one or two of the following: walnuts, pecans, seeds; plain yogurt with maple syrup drizzled on top; fresh chives, parsley, cilantro; chopped orange rind; apple pieces.

7 If you like a thinner, creamier soup, add a cup (250 ml) of low-fat milk to the pot as you reheat the soup on medium heat. Do not boil.

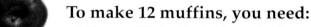

APPLE-CHEDDAR MUFFINS

This nutritious muffin is a perfect lunch dessert. It's good for you, and it tastes great! We suggest that you use whole-grain flour because it contains more nutrients and fiber than all-purpose flour does. The cornmeal adds a crunchy texture. If you like nuts, you can put a whole walnut or pecan at the top of each muffin before baking.

To make 12 muffins, you need:

- 1½ cups (375 ml) whole-grain flour such as whole wheat, oat, or spelt
- ½ cup (125 ml) cornmeal
- 1½ teaspoons (7.5 ml) baking powder
- ½ teaspoon (2.5 ml) baking soda
- 1 teaspoon (5 ml) salt
- ¾ cup (185 ml) grated cheddar cheese
- 1 cup (250 ml) chopped apple
- ¼ cup (62 ml) vegetable oil
- ⅓ cup (85 ml) granulated sugar
- 2 eggs

1 Preheat oven to 350°F (180°C). Grease the muffin tin wells with butter or line them with paper cupcake liners.

2 **Dry Mixture**: In a large mixing bowl, combine the flour, cornmeal, baking powder, baking soda, and salt.

3 **Wet mixture**: In a separate bowl, whisk together the oil and sugar and add one egg at a time.

14

4 Peel and cut the apples into bite-sized chunks. Dump the apple pieces into the dry mixture all at once and mix until they are coated.

5 Grate the cheddar and blend it into the dry mixture. Be careful not to grate your fingers!

6 Pour the wet ingredients into the dry mixture and blend well. Fill the muffin cups about half full and bake the muffins for twenty minutes. Do a toothpick test to make sure the muffins are done.

SUPER SALAD

Salad is a great addition to any meal—or it can be a meal by itself. It is full of nutrients and fiber, and it is low in fat. This salad is a treat for your taste buds and your eyes! When you see all the colors in it, you just know it will taste great. You can use the ingredients listed here or invent your own salad using your favorite veggies and other ingredients. Fresh and dried fruits, chopped boiled eggs, or a handful of nuts or grated cheese can add different textures and surprising tastes. Think of your salad as a work of art and turn your imagination loose!

You need:
- a variety of fresh greens such as spinach, arugula, and/or different kinds of lettuce greens
- 10-12 cherry or grape tomatoes or a regular tomato, diced
- red onion slices
- pepper, cucumber, celery, carrot, or radish slices
- apple, orange, or mango pieces
- a handful of raisins or dried cranberries
- a handful of nuts or seeds (Check for allergies.)

1 Wash your salad greens well and spin them dry in a salad spinner. Use as much of the lettuce as you need, depending on the number of servings you want to make. Store the rest in the refrigerator.

2 Using a salad spoon and fork, transfer your lettuce mix into your favorite salad bowl. Arrange the leaves so you have a variety of colors on top.

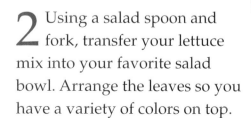

16

3 Using a sharp knife, slice or chop some peppers, tomatoes, onions, fruit, and whatever else you want to add. Lay the vegetable and fruit pieces on top of your greens—not on your face! Arrange them so your salad looks appetizing.

4 Sprinkle some nuts or seeds on your salad. Pine nuts, slivered almonds, pumpkin seeds, and sunflower seeds work great. Add raisins or dried cranberries for a delicious taste sensation!

5 To make a salad dressing for one serving of salad, use about a tablespoon each of olive oil and water, a teaspoon of raspberry vinegar, a squirt of lemon, and a shake of garlic salt or sea salt. You can take your salad to school in a plastic container but carry the salad dressing in a separate jar so your salad will not become soggy. Pour on the salad dressing just before you eat your salad. The salad on the right makes two meals or four side dishes.

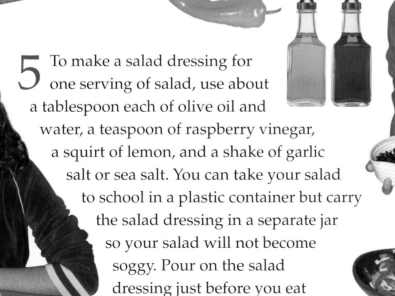

GARLIC CHICKEN BREASTS

Store-bought lunchmeats contain many ingredients that are not good for you, including salt, dyes, and chemicals such as nitrates. Slices of skinless chicken breasts make a healthier, low-fat sandwich filling, and they are an excellent source of protein. Cook them the night before if you want to eat them for lunch. They are delicious hot or cold. Remember— after you work with raw meat, wash your hands with warm water and soap and wash the counters and utensils with detergent and hot water.

You need:
- 1 teaspoon (5 ml) vegetable oil
- 2-3 boneless, skinless chicken breasts
- a pinch of salt
- a sprinkle of black pepper
- a sprinkle of paprika
- a handful of chopped parsley
- 2 garlic cloves, peeled and sliced

1 Preheat the oven to 350°F (180°C). Grease an ovenproof baking dish with the oil and spread the oil evenly. Place the chicken breasts in the dish.

2 Sprinkle salt, pepper, paprika, and parsley on the chicken breasts.

3 Peel off the outer skin of each garlic clove. Cut the garlic into thin slices. Watch your fingers!

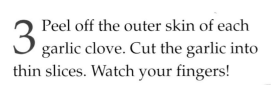

4 Bake the chicken breasts for about 40 minutes. Using oven mitts and a fork, take one of the breasts out of the oven and cut into it to make sure the meat is white, not pink inside.

5 If the chicken breasts are not cooked, bake them for another ten minutes. When they are fully cooked, take them out of the oven and allow them to cool.

6 Cut the breasts into thin slices and use them to make sandwiches, pitas, wraps, potato skins, or add them to any of the salads in this book. You can freeze the slices for up to two weeks or keep them in the refrigerator for two days.

ZESTY RICE OR PASTA SALAD

This zesty salad will wake up your taste buds after a long morning at school. The hot sauce and lemon give it an extra zing! You can make the salad using either pasta or rice, whichever you like better. If you are using rice, try brown or basmati rice. Basmati rice has a wonderful flavor! If you decide to use pasta, you can have fun trying whole-wheat or multicolored pasta in the shape of bow ties, shells, penne, or fusilli. Macaroni also works well.

For six servings you need:
- 2 cups (500 ml) cooked rice or pasta
- ½ red pepper, sliced
- ½ green pepper, sliced
- ½ red onion, sliced
- 1 tomato, diced
- 2 tablespoons (30 ml) chopped parsley
- 1 teaspoon (5 ml) olive oil

Dressing:
- ¼ cup (62 ml) olive oil
- juice of ½ lemon
- a dash of hot sauce
- a pinch of salt

1 Slice the vegetables into thin slices or dice them into bite-sized pieces, as you wish.

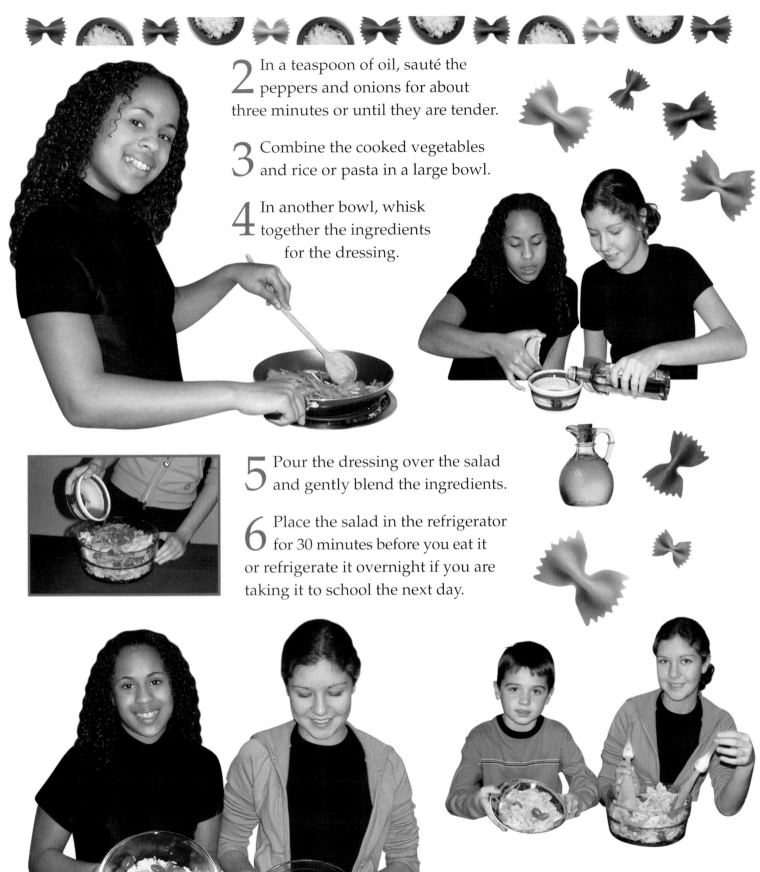

2 In a teaspoon of oil, sauté the peppers and onions for about three minutes or until they are tender.

3 Combine the cooked vegetables and rice or pasta in a large bowl.

4 In another bowl, whisk together the ingredients for the dressing.

5 Pour the dressing over the salad and gently blend the ingredients.

6 Place the salad in the refrigerator for 30 minutes before you eat it or refrigerate it overnight if you are taking it to school the next day.

rice salad

pasta salad

7 Serve the salad by itself, sprinkle cheese over it, or add some salad greens beside it on a plate. Deeelicious! Make sure you share some with your parents and friends. They'll love it, too.

21

POTATO BOATS

Potatoes contain potassium, and their skins are high in fiber. These potato skins are so loaded with good things that they look like tiny boats—which is how they got their name. They contain meat, cheese, and vegetables, so one potato is a complete meal on its own. It will keep your energy high throughout your afternoon classes. If you add salad or soup, eat only half a potato (one serving).

For four servings, you need:
- 2 baking potatoes
- one green onion, sliced
- ½ cup (125 ml) grated cheese
- ½ cup (125 ml) diced chicken breast
- ½ red or green pepper, sliced
- vegetable oil to rub on potatoes

1 Preheat the oven to 400°F (200°C). Prick the potatoes with a fork and rub them with vegetable oil. Place them in the oven in an ovenproof dish and bake for one hour.

2 To test if the potatoes are done, take one out of the oven with oven mitts and pierce it with a fork. If it is soft, take the rest of the potatoes out of the oven as well and allow them to cool.

3 Carefully cut the potato in half, lengthwise. With a teaspoon, scoop out the flesh of the potato, making a deep enough "boat" for the filling. Try not to pierce the skin of the potato. (You can use the potato flesh that you have scooped out to make mashed potatoes for another meal. Just add a little butter and a splash of milk.)

4 Carefully grate some cheese. Watch your fingers!

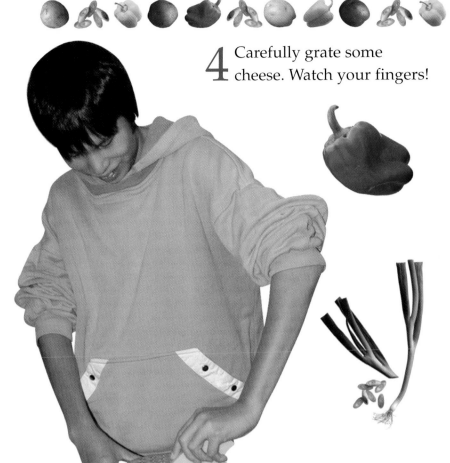

5 Cut the onion, pepper, and chicken into thin slices.

6 Spoon the sliced vegetables and meat into the potato skins and sprinkle with the grated cheese.

8 Before serving, garnish the potato boats with a bit of sour cream and a sprig of parsley.

9 Eat the potato hot at home or refrigerate it overnight to take to school. Hot or cold, Potato Boats are filling and nutritious!

7 Return the potatoes to the oven and bake them until the cheese melts.

BEAUTIFUL BEAN SALAD

Beans contain complex carbohydrates and other important nutrients such as B vitamins, vitamin C, and minerals such as iron. Eating a bean salad with a piece of whole-wheat bread provides you with a complete protein. Beans are also a great source of fiber. Rinsing the beans well will insure that you don't feel any digestive discomforts.

To make four servings, you need:
- one 19 fluid ounce (540 ml) can of mixed beans
- ½ cup (125 ml) chopped cucumber
- 1 carrot, peeled and grated
- 1 celery stalk, sliced
- ¼ cup (62 ml) diced red onion
- 1 tablespoon chopped parsley

Dressing:
- 3 tablespoons (45 ml) olive oil
- 2 tablespoons (30 ml) soy sauce
- pinch of black pepper

1 Place the beans in a colander and rinse them well under running water until there is no foam. You can see the foam in the sink stopper below.

2 Chop the cucumber, celery, parsley, and onion into small pieces.

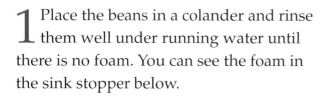

3 Peel a carrot and then grate it. Be careful not to take the skin off your fingers!

4 In a large bowl, gently stir the beans, cucumber, carrot, celery, onion, and parsley until they are mixed well.

Peel and grate like this—the safe way.

Do not grate or peel like this!

5 Add the dressing ingredients and stir them into the salad.

6 Place the salad in the refrigerator for 30 minutes to blend the flavors. Stir again.

7 Enjoy your salad with a a slice of whole-wheat or rye bread.

PITA SANDWICHES

Fish-in-a-pocket

You can use either tuna or salmon to make this yummy pita filling. Try both to see which is your favorite. Both types of fish are good for you because they contain Omega 3 fats, which protect your heart. This recipe makes enough filling to stuff two pita halves. Refrigerate any leftover filling and enjoy it the next day or make an extra pita to share with a friend at school.

You need:
- 1 small can of salmon or tuna
- 1 pickle, diced
- 1 carrot, peeled and grated
- 1 celery stalk, sliced
- 1 tablespoon (15 ml) grated parmesan cheese
- 2 tablespoons (30 ml) chopped parsley
- 1 tablespoon (15 ml) olive oil
- juice of half a lemon
- freshly grated pepper
- one whole-wheat pita
- a few lettuce leaves

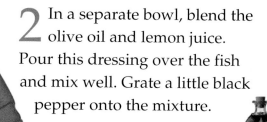

1 In a bowl, **flake**, or pull apart, the fish using a fork. Add the pickle, carrot, celery, cheese, and parsley. Mix all these ingredients together well.

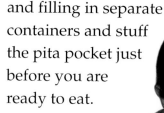

2 In a separate bowl, blend the olive oil and lemon juice. Pour this dressing over the fish and mix well. Grate a little black pepper onto the mixture.

3 Cut the pita in half. If you are ready to eat the sandwich, line it with lettuce leaves and stuff it with the filling. If you eat lunch at school, take the pita bread, lettuce, and filling in separate containers and stuff the pita pocket just before you are ready to eat.

26

Turkey pita burger

Turkey burgers make another delicious pita filling. You can also use them to fill wraps (see page 28). Have one with a side salad, and you will have a completely balanced lunch. These turkey burgers are packed with good things. They're so yummy, you'll like them better than hamburgers—and they are much lower in fat! If you like sausages, you can make the turkey taste like them by using thyme instead of cumin to spice the burgers.

For four burgers you need:

- 1 pound (0.5 kg) ground turkey
- 1 tablespoon (15 ml) vegetable oil
- ½ cup (125 ml) apple, peeled and shredded
- 1 carrot, grated
- a handful of chopped parsley
- ¼ cup (62 ml) chopped red onion
- 1 clove garlic, minced
- freshly grated pepper
- a sprinkle of cumin or thyme
- a sprinkle of salt

1 On low heat, sauté the onion, apple, and garlic in the oil for about five minutes, until they are tender. Allow them to cool for ten minutes.

2 Using a fork, blend the above ingredients and the fresh parsley into the ground turkey. Form patties. Wash your hands carefully after handling the raw meat! Cook the patties on a barbecue, an indoor grill, or under a broiler, about ten minutes on each side. Turn them gently with a spatula.

3 Cut a pita in half and line it with a lettuce leaf, as shown.

4 Cut a turkey burger in half and stuff one or both halves into your pita. Enjoy your burger with a slice of tomato and some raw onion rings. For extra flavor, add mustard or a dash of hot sauce.

27

WRAPPING IT UP

Wraps are sandwiches you make by rolling up filling in soft tortilla shells. The shells come in small and large sizes and many flavors—spinach, tomato, whole wheat, and onion, just to name a few. Tuna or salmon salad or turkey burgers make great wrap fillings, but you can put almost any food in your wrap—meat, fish, cheese, vegetables, or fruit. You can combine these ingredients in countless ways. Since the wrap is made from grain, you have at least three food groups covered! The pictures on these pages show you the secret of rolling your wrap so the filling stays inside instead of dropping all over your lap.

Making a wrap is even more fun while "rapping" with friends.

These children are using tomatoes, grated carrots, cucumbers, red pepper, lettuce, and cheese to make their wraps. The others added tuna salad (see page 26) or garlic chicken breast slices (see page 18) as well. The turkey burgers on page 27 also work well as part of a wrap filling.

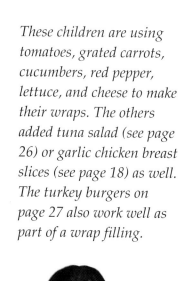

1 To make a wrap that does not leak, start with some large pieces of lettuce. For extra flavor and nutrients, add some tomato, pepper, celery, and onion slices, too.

2 Place the filling in the center of the tortilla. Your tortilla should look about half full, leaving you room to wrap.

3 To make sure nothing falls out while you are eating, fold the bottom of the wrap a third of the way up, making a pocket.

4 Next, fold one side of the wrap toward the center. Fold the other side across to make a tight roll. Nothing will fall out now!

5 The best part—eating the wrap—is yet to come! These kids have filled their wraps full of good things and are now busy munching on their delicious lunches.

29

WHAT DO I PACK FOR LUNCH?

If you are not sure what to take to school for lunch, or how much you should eat, here are some menu suggestions. Using the recipes in this book, you can make your own nutritious lunches and combine them with some other foods or drinks, as shown here.

Pack your lunch in an insulated bag so it stays cold. Take hot liquids in a Thermos. If you have meat in your lunch, you can freeze your juice and use it as an ice pack. It will thaw out by lunchtime. If you use plastic bags to pack veggies, take the bags home, wash them, and reuse them.

Menu 1
- a cup of Autumn Soup
- 1 Apple-Cheddar Muffin
- a small carton of low-fat milk (See pages 12-15.)

Menu 5
- Bean Salad
- a piece of whole-wheat bread
- Strawberry Water (See pages 7, 24-25.)

Menu 2
- Super Salad
- 1 Potato Boat
- Cucumber Water (See pages 7, 16-17, 22-23.)

Menu 6
- Pita sandwich
- a glass of low-fat milk
- a banana (See pages 26-27.)

Menu 3
- wrap made with veggies and chicken breasts
- a drink box of juice (See pages 18-19, 28-29.)

Menu 7
A picnic lunch to share
- 2 garlic chicken drumsticks (Use recipe on pages 18-19.)
- celery sticks and pepper slices
- slices of cheese
- 10-12 baby carrots
- a bunch of grapes
- orange juice

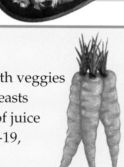

Menu 4
- Zesty Rice or Pasta
- an apple
- Orange Water (See pages 7, 20-21.)

ACTiVE AT LunchTiMe

When you eat a good lunch, you'll feel full of energy afterward. Use the energy to move your body and get active. Give yourself time to digest your food before you do anything too strenuous, such as running or jumping. If you go home for lunch, you might get your exercise by walking to and from school. If you eat lunch at school, you can go for a walk around the schoolyard, play ball with your friends, or throw a Frisbee. Near the end of your lunch break, you can run, jump rope, or spin a hula hoop. If you are active for at least twenty minutes at lunchtime, you will feel energized and be able to think much better during our afternoon classes.

Walking to and from school is great exercise!

Can you skip without stopping for fifteen minutes?

Challenge your friends to a hula-hoop contest. Who can spin the longest?

Run around the schoolyard a few times with a friend.

Stretch your body after lunch. You will feel more energetic.

31

GLOSSARY

Note: Words that have been defined in the book may not appear in the glossary. (Also see page 11 for cooking terms.)

allergy A negative reaction to certain foods

alternative A food that provides the same nutrients as another food

beta-carotene A nutrient found in red and orange vegetables, which contains Vitamin A

dehydration A dangerous lack of fluids in the body due to not drinking enough water or losing too much body fluid

digestive system A system of organs in the body that helps break down food

garnish A small edible decoration that makes food look and taste better

food groups Foods that have been divided into categories according to type

immune system A body system that fights disease and helps the body heal

legumes Dried beans

metabolic system (metabolism) A body system that changes nutrients to energy

nutritious Describing food that gives the body energy and helps it grow and heal

organic Describing foods grown or prepared without the use of harmful chemicals

processed foods Foods to which sugar, color, or other chemicals have been added

whole foods Foods that are in their natural state with very little or no processing

INDEX

apples 12, 13, 14, 15, 16, 27, 30
beans 5, 9, 24, 25
burgers 27, 28
carbohydrates 5, 24
cheese 9, 14, 15, 16, 21, 22, 23, 26, 28, 30
chicken 18, 19, 22, 23, 28, 30
  Garlic Chicken Breasts 18-19, 30
cooking terms 11
eggs 5, 9, 10, 14, 16
energy 4, 5, 6, 8, 9, 22, 31
enzymes 5, 8
fats 4, 5, 8, 16, 27
fiber 5, 8, 14, 16, 22, 24
fish 5, 9, 26, 28
food groups 8-9
fruits 4, 6, 7, 8, 10, 16, 17, 28
grains 5, 8, 13, 14, 28

meat 5, 8, 9, 10, 18, 19, 22, 23, 27, 28, 30
menus 30
milk 5, 8, 9, 13, 22, 30
minerals 5, 6, 8, 9, 24,
muffins 14, 15
  Apple-Cheddar Muffins 14-15, 30
nutrition 4-5
nutrients 5, 6, 8, 9, 12, 14, 16, 24, 28
nuts 5, 9, 10, 13, 14, 16, 17
olive oil 5, 9, 17, 20, 21, 24, 26
pasta 20, 21
pitas 19, 26, 27, 30
potatoes 19, 22, 23, 30
  Potato Boats 22-23, 30
proteins 5, 9, 18, 24

safety 10
salads 16, 17, 19, 20, 21, 22, 24, 25, 28, 27, 30
  Beautiful Bean Salad 24-25, 30
  Super Salad 16-17, 30
  Zesty Rice or Pasta Salad 20-21, 30
sandwiches 18, 19, 26, 28, 30
  Fish in a Pocket 26
  Turkey Pita Burger 27, 28
  Wraps 19, 27, 28-29, 30
soup 12, 13, 22, 30
  Autumn Soup 12, 13, 30
soy 5, 8, 9
vegetables 4, 6, 7, 8, 10, 12, 13, 16, 17, 20, 21, 22, 23, 28, 30
vitamins 5, 8, 9, 24
water 4, 5, 6-7, 10, 17, 18, 30

1 2 3 4 5 6 7 8 9 0   Printed in the U.S.A.   2 1 0 9 8 7 6 5 4 3